THE TROUBLE with the TRUTH

LEADER GUIDE
Ben Simpson, Contributor

BALANCING TRUTH AND GRACE

Nashville
Abingdon Press

THE TROUBLE WITH THE TRUTH: LEADER GUIDE

This book is printed on acid-free paper.

ISBN 978-1-4267-8626-6

14 15 16 17 18 19 20 21 22 23—10 9 8 7 6 5 4 3 2 1

MANUFACTURED IN THE UNITED STATES OF AMERICA

Contents

A Note to Group Leaders

We live in a time of increasing polarity and division. In our nation today we lack a common language or perspective concerning politics, morality, and even religion. This study asserts that polarity stems from a "trouble with the truth." We lack public consensus regarding our source and foundation for belief and action. The resulting confusion has created a divide not only in the culture but also in the church.

The purpose of *The Trouble with the Truth* is to help us clear away confusion and create a space for loving conversation. In this study we will look together at the truth—why it's in trouble, what the culture tells us about it, and why the church is so confused about it. The desired outcome is that we as Christians could become people of grace and truth, people who are like Jesus Christ. Such an outcome is possible, for Christ himself is the truth, and by his gracious power we are enabled to live as citizens in his Kingdom.

As group leader, your role is to facilitate the weekly group sessions utilizing the book *The Trouble with the Truth: Balancing Truth and Grace*, this leader guide, and the DVD. This guide includes detailed instructions for six one-hour group sessions. (If you would like to extend the group session to 90 minutes, simply increase the time allowed for group discussion and prayer.)

Each session outline has four primary sections:

1. Charting the Course
2. Getting Started
3. Engaging the Material
4. Closing the Session

In "Charting the Course," you will find a learning objective, themes for exploration, a key Scripture, and a theological focus. "Getting Started" equips you with an opening prayer and conversation starter. Then, "Engaging the Material" provides summary statements and questions that foster interaction with the video, the Scriptures, and the book, as well as an application activity that participants can undertake between group sessions. Finally, "Closing the Session" provides a final statement and a written prayer to bring the session to a close.

As you prepare to lead each group session, be sure to thoroughly read and reflect upon the lesson plan and corresponding chapter in the book, as well as view the video segment. Given the topics and themes addressed in this study, it is not advisable to show up cold and unprepared. Proverbs 12:18 says, "Some chatter on like a stabbing sword, / but a wise tongue heals" (CEB). Familiarity with the content will help you carefully measure your words in presenting the material. For some, truth may be a difficult topic. Some of your group members will have people they love with whom they disagree on important topics, and the wounds may be fresh. This study is an opportunity to model the balance of truth and grace, foster growth in Christlike character, and invite the healing power of God to unify rather than divide. The skills we will gain in becoming people of grace and truth are meant to help us navigate the most difficult questions facing Christians today and to do so with love.

Lastly, remember that by leading this study you are being faithful to Jesus' command to teach and disciple others. Remain positive and never forget that the Lord is with you. Ask for his help. As you do so, constantly point to him as the perfect embodiment of grace and truth. Despite our shortcomings, he is always faithful. Follow him as he calls, and invite others to do the same.

Leader Helps

Preparing for the Session

- Ask the Holy Spirit for help as you prepare for the study. Pray for discernment for each member of the group, including yourself.
- Before each session, familiarize yourself with the book content. Consider reading the chapter again. Prescreen the video segment.
- Choose the session elements you will use during the group session, including the specific discussion questions you will cover. Be prepared to adjust the session as group members interact and questions arise. Allow for the Holy Spirit to move in and through the material, the group members, and you.
- Secure a TV and a DVD player prior to the session. Test all your connections and video playback before group participants arrive.
- Arrange the meeting space to enhance the learning process. Group members should be seated around a table or in a circle so that all can see each other. Moveable chairs are best, because the group will occasionally form pairs or small groups of 3 to 5 for discussion.
- Bring Bibles for those who forget to bring one or who might not have one. (If someone is reading aloud, you might ask the person to identify from which Bible translation he or she is reading.)

- Encourage participants to bring a journal or notebook. Have paper and pens or pencils available.
- You may want access to a chalkboard, whiteboard, or an easel. If your teaching style includes recording responses from participants or writing questions or quotations for discussion on a board, make sure your gathering space has these tools available, with adequate chalk or markers.

Shaping the Learning Environment

- Provide participants with a class schedule. In order to maintain continuity, it would be best if your class meets for six consecutive weeks.
- Each lesson plan outlines a 60-minute session. Because the video, Bible, and book material could lead to substantial discussion, you may need to make choices in what you will cover; or you may choose to extend your group sessions to 90 minutes to allow more time for discussion.
- Create a climate where it is safe to share. Encourage group members to participate as they feel comfortable. Remember that some will be eager to give answers or offer commentary, while others will need time to process and think.
- If you notice that some participants are reticent to enter the conversation, ask if they have thoughts to share. Give everyone an opportunity to talk, but keep the conversation moving. Intervene when necessary to prevent a few individuals from dominating discussion.
- Stress the importance of group discussions and group exercises. We are seeking wisdom from one another.
- If no one answers at first during a discussion, do not be afraid of silence. Count silently to ten; then say, "Would anyone like to go first?" If no one responds, provide your own answer and ask for reactions. If you limit your sharing to a surface level,

others will follow suit. Keep in mind that if your group is new, cohesion might take a couple of weeks to form. If group members do not share at first, give them time.

- Model openness as you share with the group. Group members will follow your example.
- Encourage multiple answers or responses before moving on.
- Ask, "Why?" or "Why do you believe that?" or "Can you say more about that?" to draw out greater depth from a response.
- Affirm others' responses with comments such as "Great" or "Thanks" or "Good insight"—especially if this is the first time someone has spoken during the group session.
- Monitor your own contributions. If you are doing most of the talking, back off so that you do not train the group to listen rather than speak.
- Try to ask questions that are open ended. If you do ask a closed "yes or no" question, follow it with a request for explanation.
- Remember that you do not have all the answers, and that is okay. Your job is to keep the discussion going and encourage participation. If you do not know the answer to a particular question, tell the group that you will try to find out. Write it down. Ask a pastor for help, or do some research.

Managing Time, Participation, and Confidentiality

- Honor the designated time window. Begin on time. If a session runs longer than expected, get consensus from the group before continuing.
- Involve participants in various aspects of the session, such as playing the DVD, offering prayer, and reading Scripture.
- Do not make anyone participate who does not want to. If you have someone who is hesitant to share, you might ask the individual informally for his or her thoughts on the study before or after your session. Then, if the individual shares something

of relevance, thank the person and ask if he or she would be willing to offer that same thought in the next group session.

- Note that the session guides sometime call for small discussion groups. This discusison gives everyone a chance to speak and participate fully. You might want to mix up the groupings, or allow people to stay together consistently in order to develop friendships.

- Because some activities call for personal sharing, confidentiality is essential. Remind group members at each session of the importance of confidentiality and of not passing along stories that have been shared in the group.

Session 1
Full of Grace and Truth

Charting the Course

Learning Objective

Participants will examine the truth-grace dynamic revealed in Christ and begin pursuit of the proper balance of truth and grace in their lives.

Themes for Exploration

- We see the perfect combination of grace and truth in the life of Jesus.
- To walk as Jesus walked, we must balance grace and truth.
- The culture and the church influence our beliefs about grace and truth.

Key Scripture

The Word became flesh and made his dwelling among us. We have seen his glory, the glory of the one and only Son, who came from the Father, full of grace and truth.

John 1:14

Theological Focus

"When the Father sent the Son into the world that we might be saved, he came with grace and truth, compassion and righteousness, love and holiness. Without grace and truth together, we don't have the God of the Bible. Without compassion and righteousness together, we don't have Jesus of the Gospels. Without love and holiness together, we don't have the good news. The Christian faith is not one instead of the other or one more than the other but both together in equal measure, because this is the nature of our God."

Getting Started (10 Minutes)

Opening Prayer

Almighty God, together we seek to be faithful disciples of Jesus. May we behold him, filled with grace and truth. May we see that in him, a life is possible where compassion and righteousness, love and holiness, and justice and mercy can be held in tandem. Help us to hold fast to his teachings and to follow his example. In Jesus' name. Amen.

Conversation Starter

Say:

The first chapter in our book explores grace and truth as vital attributes of Christian character. In our world, and even in our church cultures, we tend to favor one over the other rather than seeking both in equal measure. Today we will discuss how these attributes were displayed by Jesus and consider how we might grow as people of grace and truth.

Ask:

- What individual do you know who exudes grace? What is he or she like? How have you seen this person affect the lives of others?
- What individual do you know who has a contagious love for truth, sharing it in a positive and impactful way?

Engaging the Material (40 Minutes)

Note: This section allows approximately 25 minutes total for discussion (of video, Scriptures, and book). More questions are provided than you will have time to cover; select in advance those questions you would like to discuss, putting a check mark beside each one.

The Video

Play: Session 1: Full of Grace and Truth (running time 12:21)

Discuss:

- Why is it essential for us as Christians to be people of both grace and truth?
- How does the example of Nik Wallenda, who walked on a high wire across the Little Colorado River Gorge, speak to us about balancing grace and truth?
- In the midst of a culture that influences us so greatly, how can we get God's values into our minds and hearts?
- Would you agree that there are times when the kindest, most compassionate thing we can do is speak truth to someone? Why or why not? If so, give an example.

The Scriptures

In Advance: Use a commentary or Bible dictionary to help you prepare for this segment. Become familiar with the text before the group session begins. Write down your own discussion questions in addition to those provided below.

Read Aloud: John 8:1-11

Discuss:

- What takes place in this passage? Who is present? What is the crisis or dilemma? Who are Jesus' opponents?
- What was the prevailing cultural attitude of the crowd?
- How does Jesus demonstrate grace and truth in this passage?
- What does his example teach us?

Conclude by reading John 1:14 aloud. Explain that following Christ should lead to a life of grace and truth. Jesus displayed both through his words and his actions. As followers of Jesus, we must do the same.

The Book

Chapter 1 presents two essential qualities displayed in the life of Jesus: grace and truth. The current preference in Western culture seems to be for grace over truth. But Jesus offers a different image, a perfect balance of grace and truth. Christ's compassion was rooted in his strong and certain knowledge of his Father's love. We must ask him to teach us how to be people who, like him, are full of grace and truth. We must resist the influence of our culture to emphasize one over the other.

Discuss:

- What does the life of Christ teach us about grace and truth?
- Do you agree that the winds of our current culture encourage us to lean more toward compassion than truth? Why or why not?
- In what ways has the culture influenced your beliefs about grace and truth?
- Think of your church community. Is grace emphasized more than truth or vice versa? What about the church of your formative years? Discuss with a partner or small group how these experiences have shaped your understanding of grace and truth.
- Are you a more of a "truther" or a "gracer"? Share with your partner or small group how this tendency is a strength, and explore where you have room to grow.
- How can we best respond to other Christians who balance truth and grace differently than we do?
- Have someone read the following aloud: "What might happen if the church of Jesus Christ was not afraid to love like Jesus and was not ashamed to speak the truth like Jesus? His grace and truth changed the world once before. And I believe if we get it right, his grace and truth can change the world again through us." What might this look like in your church and community?

Life Application

Say:

Becoming a person of grace and truth requires us to face who we are today. If possible, try to find time this week to sit down with a friend you trust; this person should be a mature Christian who knows you well. Share what you are exploring in this study and explore these questions together (note: instruct participants to jot these down as you read them, or write them on a board or chart):

1. How do I show grace?
2. How do I proclaim truth?
3. Do I demonstrate grace and truth equally, or do I tend to favor one over the other?
4. What specific actions can I take that will help me grow as a person of grace and truth?

Be open and teachable. Listen, being willing to accept hard words if they come. Proverbs 27:6 says, "Wounds from a friend can be trusted, / but an enemy multiplies kisses." Do not be defensive. The goal is to become a person of grace and truth in equal measure, like Jesus.

Proverbs 27:17 says, "As iron sharpens iron, / so one person sharpens another." Through your friend, you will gain self-knowledge that will assist your spiritual growth and inform your prayer life as you ask God for help.

If you are unable to do this exercise with a friend, devote some time to an honest self-evaluation. Ask these questions of yourself, seeking God's discernment through prayer.

Closing the Session (10 Minutes)

A Final Reflection

Say:

Blaise Pascal once remarked, "Nothing gives rest but the sincere search for truth."[1] Christians believe that ultimately, truth is not a proposition but a person, Jesus Christ. When we find him, we find not only rest but also immeasurable grace extended toward us, warming our hearts, washing away our sin, and giving us power to live in accordance with the will of God. Grace and truth belong together in us, and it is God's desire to shape us as people of both compassion and conviction. Let us ask God to teach us to be faithful disciples.

Closing Prayer

Lord Jesus, we ask for your help. You walked among us, full of grace and truth. Change us by the power of the Holy Spirit so that your life might be made manifest in us. Direct our words, our actions, and the inclination of our hearts so that we may bring glory to our Father who dwells in the heavens, who has called us as children, and who has created us for good works. Let us hold steadfast to truth and remain gracious toward all people. Amen.

Session 2
Why Grace Is Essential and Truth Matters

Charting the Course

Learning Objective

Participants will understand the biblical foundation for grace and truth and discuss real-life situations when it is challenging to embody grace and truth.

Themes for Exploration

- Grace is essential because Jesus commanded it and lived it; compassion was central to all that he did.
- Grace enables people to hear the truth; they don't care how much we know until they know how much we care.
- Truth is required for spiritual and emotional growth.
- Truth matters because our beliefs determine our lives.
- Truth dispels lies and combats evil.

Key Scripture

Now the tax collectors and sinners were all gathering around to hear Jesus. But the Pharisees and the teachers of the law muttered, "This man welcomes sinners and eats with them."

Luke 15:1-2

Theological Focus

"If we are to have an impact on our world the way Jesus did, then we must possess his compassion for people and his passion for truth. Both are equally important for those of us who want to represent him well and care for people the way he did."

Getting Started (10 Minutes)

Opening Prayer

Holy God, you are our Creator. We thank you for making us and calling us into being. We pray that you would help us to see how grace is essential. We must be people of compassion, for you are a God of compassion. Help us also to see that truth matters. Truth has the power to liberate and heal us. Let us trust you to sanctify us in truth, soften our hearts, and be with us as we engage in your work. We ask that you do these things through the power of the Holy Spirit. Amen.

Conversation Starter

In preparation for this session, look for a story of forgiveness in print media, on the Internet, or from daily life. Share the details of the story with the group.

Ask:

- How was grace demonstrated in this particular case? How did an individual or individuals show compassion for someone who wronged or hurt them?
- What convictions led those involved to act as they did? How did truth make a difference in this situation?

Alternate Option: Ask participants to share any experiences they've had related to grace and truth since your last gathering. What has God been teaching you? How have you been learning to show grace? How have you been learning to arrive at your convictions or speak truth?

Engaging the Material (40 Minutes)

Note: This section allows approximately 25 minutes total for discussion (of video, Scriptures, and book). More questions are provided than you will have time to cover; select in advance those questions you would like to discuss, putting a check mark beside each one.

The Video

Play: Session 2: Why Grace Is Essential and Truth Matters (running time 15:17)

Discuss:

- How would you explain why grace is foundational to the Christian faith?
- How do we see grace and compassion at the heart of Jesus' ministry?
- Why is looking at the truth of who God is and who we are necessary if we want to grow spiritually?
- Is there an untruth commonly accepted by our culture that you feel compelled to address in some way? What is it, and how can you address it?
- As Christians, how can we express our convictions in a manner that is humble, grace-filled, and compassionate?

- What does it mean to say that love is the ultimate apologetic?
- When has someone demonstrated compassion by speaking the truth that you needed to hear? How did it make a difference in your life?

The Scriptures

In Advance: Use a commentary or Bible dictionary to help you prepare for this segment. Become familiar with the text before the group session. Write down your own discussion questions in addition to those provided below.

Read Aloud: Luke 15:1-2, 11-32

Discuss:

- What is taking place in the beginning of this passage? Who is present? What is the crisis or dilemma? Who are Jesus' opponents?
- What was the prevailing cultural attitude of the crowd?
- How does Jesus demonstrate grace and truth in verse 1? in the parable that he tells?
- What does his example teach us?

This teaching is often remembered as a profound statement concerning the grace of God, and it is arguably Jesus' best-known parable. The focus is often on the younger brother. Like those gathered to hear Jesus, he was a known "sinner." We are drawn to the image of the father welcoming home his wayward son with grace.

But Jesus is also teaching another lesson. Take a few moments to focus on Luke 15:1-2, 28-32. Jesus speaks a very direct word of truth, conveyed through story, to the "older brothers" who grumbled against Jesus' acceptance of tax collectors and sinners.

Jesus rebukes those who are self-righteous toward those outside of their circle. The Pharisees and legal experts favored truth over grace. In this parable, Jesus tells us that both are invited to the feast. The question before truthers and gracers is whether we will come in and celebrate with the Father.

The Book

Chapter 2 directs our attention to the Bible, highlighting the importance of both grace and truth. Related to grace, we see that compassion and love are central to the Christian gospel, that Jesus was motivated by compassion and commanded us to extend grace, that "truth without love is a lie," and that grace can open someone to truth. Related to truth, we see that truth promotes and stimulates growth, that ideas have consequences, that lies can become accepted as reality, and that truth ultimately leads to victory over evil. The final judge of our faithfulness is God, who calls us to be people of grace and truth.

Discuss:

- Do you agree that grace and truth are not in competition? Why or why not? How can they be partners in creating a beautiful life that looks like the life of Jesus? What is your understanding of how grace and truth work together? Give a few concrete examples.
- When you were growing up, did you view God as more loving or more judgmental? Why? Has your view of God changed, and if so, why?
- How do our ideas about God impact how we relate to other people? What difference does it make in our lives for us to understand God's perfect love and God's position as our judge (arbiter of truth)?

- Which played more of a role in the way that you came to faith in Christ—grace or truth?
- When have you seen or heard someone speak the truth in a way that was judgmental or harsh? What made it that way? How did the recipient respond?
- How can we discern when to speak the truth boldly and when to remain silent?
- When are truth claims most likely to be met with controversy? Are there times when an expression of grace might be seen as inappropriate, even if right?
- What role does the Holy Spirit play in teaching us to be people of grace and truth?
- As disciples of Jesus, how do we gracefully navigate hot-button issues like abortion, human sexuality, war and peace, the environment, politics, and so forth?

Life Application

Say:

This week, spend time with a Bible and a journal. Focus on a single instance of grace or compassion you find in Scripture. Select this passage using a concordance, or choose one of the suggested Scriptures. Spend time thinking and meditating on these words. Write your reflections in your journal. Ask God to use the words of Scripture to transform your mind. Then, do the same with a passage of Scripture that speaks the importance of truth.

Note: Have participants jot down one or more of the following suggested passages as you name them, or write them on a board or chart.

Suggested Passages on Grace: Matthew 9:36-38; Luke 10:30-35; 2 Corinthians 12:8-9; Ephesians 2:4-9; Colossians 3:12; Hebrews 4:16; 1 Peter 5:10

Suggested Passages on Truth: Psalm 25:5; Psalm 119:160; John 1:17; John 8:32; John 17:17; Ephesians 4:15; 2 Timothy 2:15

Closing the Session (10 Minutes)

A Final Reflection

Say:

Christian missionary Hudson Taylor once claimed, "God's work done in God's way will never lack God's supplies."[2] For some of us, becoming people of grace and truth may be challenging. There are many who suffer, and our world is in need of compassion. We live in turbulent times, and our world is in need of people who confidently proclaim truth. We do not have all the answers, but we do follow Christ. Let us seek to do his work and trust that in his Kingdom, he will give us the resources we need to serve him faithfully.

Closing Prayer

Gracious God of truth, may your will be done on this earth as it is in heaven. We confess our inadequacies and failures, for we have not always faithfully answered your call to show compassion or to speak truthfully. Help us as we go forth. Renew our minds so that we might know your will, and guide our hands and feet as we seek to do your work. In Jesus' name. Amen.

Session 3
Why Our Culture Values Compassion Over Truth: Understanding Three Worldviews

Charting the Course

Learning Objective

Participants will explore three basic worldviews and examine them in light of our current culture.

Themes for Exploration

- A worldview is a lens through which we perceive reality and make sense of the world.
- A scriptural worldview asserts that there are spiritual and moral truths that apply to everyone, and that these truths have been revealed to us by God in his Word and in the person of Jesus Christ.
- A modern worldview asserts that human beings have the intellectual capacity to determine and prove what is moral and true through the power of reason, logic, and science. Modernism removes God from the reality of daily life.

- Protestant Liberalism was born through the influence of modernism.
- A postmodern worldview asserts that theological and moral beliefs are valid if they are meaningful to the person who holds them; truth is subjective and relative.

Key Scripture

> *Let my request for grace come before you;*
>   *deliver me according to your promise!*
>
> Psalm 119:170 CEB

Theological Focus

"A worldview is a lens through which we perceive reality and make sense of the world. It's a set of assumptions, beliefs, and values we use to determine the meaning of our experiences and the validity of competing truth claims. Since the early days of Christianity, there has been a progression from a scriptural worldview to a modern worldview to a postmodern worldview. Understanding each of these worldviews will give us greater insight into why there is such trouble with the truth today."

Getting Started (10 Minutes)

Opening Prayer

Holy Spirit, we believe that you are always at work. You are drawing people to God, even today, changing hearts and transforming lives, guiding the church, and offering comfort to the sorrowful and weary. May we be among those you comfort;

we need you to still our hearts. Our world is in chaos, and we are concerned. Help us to understand our world, and the way that people throughout time have understood it, so that we might more faithfully serve Jesus Christ. Amen.

Conversation Starter

Provide each participant with a piece of paper and a pen or pencil. Ask everyone to think of a particular tree in his or her past or present that is special for some reason. Have them hold that image in their minds. Then, ask everyone to draw a picture of the tree.

Say:

Everyone has a unique set of experiences that form his or her perceptions and way of understanding the world. The images you have drawn are representations of an encounter or an experience that you have had and what you have seen with your own eyes. Maybe you love this tree because it was fitted with a tire swing from your childhood, it provided you with shade on a hot day, or it was the place of your first kiss. You look on this image with spectacles or glasses that make this your favorite tree. The tree itself is real—it is a fixture in reality. But the meaning you ascribe to this tree is filtered through circumstances from your own life.

As human beings, we are constantly faced with the realities of our world—war, strife, times of peace, experiences of beauty. We are simultaneously seeking to come to grips with what is real and to derive meaning from our experiences. We are always forming and shaping our worldview. As Christians, our calling is to learn to see the world as God sees it and to work according to his purposes. Today we will examine how people have understood

31

reality throughout time and seek to align our worldview according to Christ's calling.

Alternate Option: Ask participants to share one of the verses of Scripture they have meditated on since your last session (a grace Scripture or a truth Scripture) and what they have learned as they have listened to God.

Engaging the Material (40 Minutes)

Note: This section allows approximately 25 minutes total for discussion (of video, Scriptures, and book). More questions are provided than you will have time to cover; select in advance those questions you would like to discuss, putting a check mark beside each one.

The Video

Play: Session 3: Why Our Culture Values Compassion Over Truth (running time 11:48)

Discuss:

- How does a basic understanding of the history of Western thought help us understand our current culture?
- Why is there such confusion about truth in our culture today?
- In what ways do we see the same struggle to determine what is true within the church that we see within the culture?
- Would you agree that if you emphasize grace without holding on to the essential truth claims of the gospel, you no longer have true Christianity? Why or why not?

- As Christians, how can we live and witness faithfully in a church that often seems unwilling to stand up for the very truths that Jesus was willing to die for?

The Scriptures

In Advance: Use a commentary or Bible dictionary to help you prepare for this segment. Become familiar with the text before the group session. Write down your own discussion questions in addition to those provided below.

Read Aloud: Psalm 119:169-176

Ask:

- This psalm is a meditation on God's commandments and how they lead us in living a life with God. Where does the writer mention or ask for grace? Where does the writer claim truth, and how does this give us confidence to face our challenges?
- How does the psalmist see and understand the world? How have God's commandments impacted and defined the psalmist's worldview?
- How does the study of Scripture shape our worldview?

The Book

Chapter 3 explores the concept of worldview. A worldview is "a lens through which we perceive reality and make sense of the world." This chapter explores three worldviews: scriptural, modern, and postmodern. The chapter outlines these three views, identifies the challenges modernism and postmodernism pose for Christianity, and helps us understand the world we are seeking to faithfully serve.

Discuss:

- What is a worldview? How do we form our worldview? How do we engage with someone who has a different worldview?
- How would you characterize or describe a scriptural worldview?
- How does the explosion of Christianity in the first four centuries lend credibility to its claim to be true?
- How would you characterize or describe a modern worldview?
- Would you agree with the statement that modernism cannot make sense of what makes us human? Why or why not? How does Christianity make sense of our world in a way modernism does not?
- How would you characterize or describe a postmodern worldview?
- How has American culture—including values and behaviors—changed during your lifetime? Give some examples. Which of these changes do you see as positive and which do you see as negative? What helps you decide if a change is God-honoring or contrary to the values of God's kingdom?
- What cultural influences have contributed to the changes you identified? Behind these influences, do you see a shift in how our culture thinks about spiritual and moral truth? If so, how would you describe this shift?
- In what ways are many people—including many in the church—influenced to see spiritual truth as nothing more than individual preferences? How have you seen this in your life? How might you respond to someone who thinks faith is simply a matter of personal, private preferences?
- Do you agree that postmodernism is a threat to the church and its proclamation of the gospel? Why or why not?
- What is the role of the church in teaching and instructng people in scriptural truth? How must we as the body of Christ live if the church is to give credibility to the worldview it proclaims?

Life Application

Say:

This week pay attention to the worldview or views you encounter as you go about your daily life—listening to the radio, watching TV, reading the newspaper, browsing the Internet. What are they? How are they evident? What questions do they raise? As you become more aware of the worldview or views being expressed all around you, seek answers within Christianity that will enhance your witness to God's grace and truth.

Closing the Session (10 Minutes)

A Final Reflection

Say:

We live within our understanding of reality, and so do our neighbors. Therefore, we are first called to examine our own worldview and seek God's assistance in aligning our viewpoint in accord with Scripture and sound theological reflection. Second, we must remember that to love our neighbors well, we must first listen and understand. We must be people of grace if we are to compel and persuade others to discover God's great love for us.

Closing Prayer

God, we have read in Scripture that you have so loved the world, you gave your only Son, and that all who trust him will have life eternal. It is our prayer that all people, including your church, would be given the eyes to see this is true. Knowing that you love us is a life-changing truth, a worldview-shaping truth. Help us not only to know and understand our world, but to know you so that we might serve you as true disciples. We ask this in Jesus' name. Amen.

Session 4
Comparing the Cultural Worldview to a Scriptural Worldview

Charting the Course

Learning Objective

Participants will explore a scriptural worldview and weigh scriptural truth in comparison with a cultural worldview.

Themes for Exploration

- A scriptural worldview sees spiritual and moral truth as objective and universal; it believes truth is determined by God and applies to everyone.
- Postmoderism believes that truth is subjective, relative, and situational; there are no overarching truths that provide a moral compass for all.
- We are guilty of idolatry when we believe that who God is—and what is morally true—is determined by our reason and experiences.
- If morality is based on God's nature and character and God's character does not change, then what is morally true does not change.

Key Scripture

Therefore, I urge you, brothers and sisters, in view of God's mercy, to offer your bodies as a living sacrifice, holy and pleasing to God—this is your true and proper worship. Do not conform to the pattern of this world, but be transformed by the renewing of your mind. Then you will be able to test and approve what God's will is—his good, pleasing and perfect will.

Romans 12:1-2

Theological Focus

"A scriptural worldview sees spiritual/moral truth as objective and universal. It believes truth is determined by God and applies to everyone."

Getting Started (10 Minutes)

Note: In advance of the group session, read and evaluate the Conversation Starter for Session 4. If you choose the first option (rather than the alternate), you may wish to proceed with that exercise before offering the following opening prayer. Do what is best for your group.

Opening Prayer

Lord, our minds absorb ideas and assumptions about reality like a sponge soaks up a spill. Our world can lead us astray. Purify our thoughts and transform our minds. Bring us back to you. Establish your story in our lives so that we live according to its truth. Rid us of falsehood; please do so by your grace. Help us to be effective witnesses to Jesus Christ. We ask these things by the power of his name. Amen.

Conversation Starter

Bring a large sponge and a bowl of water to your session. Place them before the class. Drop the sponge in the bowl.

Say:

Many of our beliefs about reality are picked up from our environment. Often we do not consciously reflect upon how we know what we know, or why we behave as we do. Sometimes we can be like a sponge, soaking up whatever we are around.

Ask:

What are some ways we absorb beliefs and practices from our environment like a sponge soaks up water? How does the study of Scripture or meeting with other Christians for fellowship and worship shape us as faithful disciples? What do we soak up when we do those things?

Say:

Today we are going to talk about the differences between a scriptural worldview and a cultural worldview and how we ground ourselves in the story of God.

Alternate Option: Have group members share any observations they made about worldviews being expressed around them during the previous week. Where did group members see the scriptural, modern, or postmodern views operative in mass media or daily life?

Engaging the Material (40 Minutes)

Note: This section allows approximately 25 minutes total for discussion (of video, Scriptures, and book). More questions are provided than you will have time to cover; select in advance those questions you would like to discuss, putting a check mark beside each one.

The Video

Play: Session 4: Comparing the Cultural Worldview to a Scriptural Worldview (running time 10:53)

Discuss:

- How would you respond to this statement? There are universal truths that apply to all people, at all times, and in all places.
- In what ways and to what degree are you a mixture of a scriptural worldview and a cultural worldview?
- How can the influence of the cultural worldview subtly affect our heart for evangelism?
- What does Christianity offer that our culture cannot provide? How can we draw others to Jesus Christ by the way we live?

The Scriptures

In Advance: Use a commentary or Bible dictionary to help you prepare for this segment. Become familiar with the text before the group session. Write down your own discussion questions in addition to those provided below.

Read: Romans 12:1-2

Ask:

- Who was Paul writing to? How does Paul invite his readers to be different?
- What does this passage say concerning our minds? How do we change our thought patterns in a way that aligns with God's will?
- What does this passage say concerning our bodies? How is our worldview reflected in what we do with our bodies? How does a scriptural worldview affect our ability to resist temptation, control anger and other emotions, remain at peace, and serve others?
- How does this passage challenge a postmodern worldview?

The Book

Chapter 4 compares postmodern and scriptural worldviews. The key is to remember the centrality of a scriptural worldview for the Christian disciple. Review the differences between these two worldviews with those in your group.

Discuss:

- How would you compare and contrast a scriptural worldview and a postmodern worldview? What are the primary differences?
- How do we sometimes shape God into what we want him to be, remaking him into our God *du jour*? Why is this dangerous?
- Do you believe it is wrong for us as Christians to deny that there are universal rights and wrongs? Why or why not?
- What is the difference between imposing our values on others and desiring others to embrace a Kingdom way of life? Why is this distinction important? What does it look like to encourage others to embrace a Kingdom way of life following the example of Jesus?

- What does it mean to say that although we believe there are absolute truths, we do not have the truth absolutely? Why is this important for us to acknowledge?
- Who are some Christian leaders who are effective conveyers of a scriptural worldview? What makes them effective?

Life Application

Say:

Romans 12:1-2 says:

Therefore, I urge you, brothers and sisters, in view of God's mercy, to offer your bodies as a living sacrifice, holy and pleasing to God— this is your true and proper worship. Do not conform to the pattern of this world, but be transformed by the renewing of your mind. Then you will be able to test and approve what God's will is—his good, pleasing and perfect will.

This week, memorize this passage of Scripture. Write it on a note card and carry it with you. Say it out loud. Ask someone to help you review the passage.

Closing the Session (10 Minutes)

A Final Reflection

Say:

In her book *Bird by Bird*, Anne Lamott quotes her priest friend Tom, who says, "You can safely assume you've created God in your own image when it turns out that God hates all the same people you do."[3] It would be quite possible for us, in our rejection of a cultural view, to assume we are somehow superior to those who do not possess a scriptural outlook on reality. But as Christians, we do not believe we have been saved because of our worldview nor that we have arrived at a scriptural worldview because we are better or smarter than other people. We believe we have been saved by grace! As we come to a greater understanding of God and his mercy, as our minds are transformed and we are able to discern God's will, let us show forth the same grace that has been given to us in Jesus Christ so that the world may see the truth.

Closing Prayer

Father, Son, and Holy Spirit, you have given us Scripture so that we might know you and the salvation you have made possible through Jesus. Renew our minds so that we might be able to know your will, and give us the grace to do it. Strip away our self-righteousness, and let us put our full confidence in you. You have redeemed us so that we might be a light in the darkness. Let us glorify you. Amen.

Session 5
The New Absolutes

Charting the Course

Learning Objective

Participants will explore the "new absolutes" of openness, tolerance, pluralism, and nonjudgmentalism and develop a Christian nuance on these ideas.

Themes for Exploration

- Openness traditionally has meant "that we hold our views with humility, acknowledging that we have much to learn"; but "the New Openness insists that we must accept all beliefs—all ideas, theories, or convictions—as equally valid."
- Tolerance has traditionally been understood "as a willingness to let people be who they are, think what they think, and say what they want to say—even if we disagree. . . . Today's tolerance requires that you embrace and even celebrate the other person's moral choices and lifestyle as being good and right."
- Pluralism is the belief "that the world's religions are equally valid paths for approaching God."

- Jesus' love "did not prevent him from telling people when their beliefs were wrong and their actions were sinful."
- Being nonjudgmental used to mean "respectfully disagreeing with another person after considering his or her views"; today it means never questioning another person's beliefs or actions.

Key Scripture

> "My thoughts are not your thoughts,
>   neither are your ways my ways,"
>   declares the LORD.
> "As the heavens are higher than the earth,
>   so are my ways higher than your ways
>   and my thoughts than your thoughts."

Isaiah 55:8-9

Theological Focus

"We can deny it with our heads, but our hearts yearn for something big enough to live for and solid enough to stand on. And those of us who know that the answer is a living relationship with the God of the universe through faith in Jesus Christ must not—out of fear or a need to be thought politically correct—keep the truth from a world that desperately needs to hear it. Love requires that we balance grace and truth."

Getting Started (10 Minutes)

Opening Prayer

Jesus, many of our neighbors have an outlook on openness, tolerance, pluralism, and nonjudgment that makes it difficult for some of us to speak truth with confidence. Help us to understand the "New Absolutes" and to think how, as Christians, we can live these values in a way that is faithful to you and more deeply loving toward our neighbor. By your grace, grant us the boldness we need to share the gospel message: that you came to this earth, died, and were resurrected; and that through trusting you we can receive forgiveness of sin and live with you forever. Amen.

Conversation Starter

To begin class, choose a public example of a debate surrounding openness, tolerance, pluralism, or nonjudgmentalism. Share the details of the example with the group.

Ask:

How should we react to this example as followers of Jesus?

Alternate Option: Contact your class a few days before your group session, and ask them to bring examples of the New Absolutes they find in print media, on the Internet, or from daily life. Divide the class into small groups, and give them a few minutes to share and discuss their examples.

Engaging the Material (40 Minutes)

Note: This section allows approximately 25 minutes total for discussion (of video, Scriptures, and book). More questions are provided than you will have time to cover; select in advance those questions you would like to discuss, putting a check mark beside each one.

The Video

Play: Session 5: The New Absolutes (running time 12:51)

Discuss:

- What are absolute truths?
- What is the difference between believing in absolute truths and believing you have the truth absolutely? How can we hold on to absolute truths while at the same time realizing we may need to grow and see some things differently?
- What is "new" about the New Absolutes: openness, tolerance, pluralism, and being nonjudgmental?
- How do the religions of the world define the human problem differently? How does Christianity define the human problem, and what answer does it provide?
- How is humility the cardinal virtue of the Christian faith?

The Scriptures

In Advance: Use a commentary or Bible dictionary to help you prepare for this segment. Become familiar with the text before the group session. Write down your own discussion questions in addition to those provided below.

Read: Luke 7:36-50

Ask:

- What takes place in this passage? Who is Jesus dining with, who is the woman, and what is the controversy?
- How does Jesus exhibit grace? To whom does he speak truth?
- How does Jesus show us a different posture toward grace and truth in this passage?
- How does Jesus help us see what it means to be truly open, loving, and accepting of the other? How does his grace transform this woman, and how does his truth-telling challenge the social conventions of the Pharisee and his friends?

- In what ways does God challenge and show us that his way is not always our way, nor his plans our plans?

The Book

Chapter 5 identifies four public virtues referred to as the New Absolutes: openness, tolerance, pluralism, and nonjudgmentalism. This chapter challenges postmodern definitions of these cultural virtues and invites Christians to engage more fully with the heart of the gospel in a way that transcends postmodern notions of acceptance.

Discuss:

- What is the New Openness, and how does it compare to the traditional understanding of openness?
- What is the New Tolerance, and how does it compare to the traditional understanding of tolerance?
- Respond to the following statement: Tolerance is easy; love is difficult. What is the difference between love and tolerance? What does it mean to say that Christian love goes beyond tolerance?
- When is it appropriate to share our beliefs with someone we consider to be mistaken in his or her views? How can we do this in a sensitive, loving way without causing offense?
- How can we act lovingly toward someone whom we are convinced is making destructive choices?
- How can we faithfully relate to persons of other religious beliefs, or those who are committed skeptics?
- How would you explain the difference between judgment and condemnation?

- Do you believe an individual is being intolerant or uncaring if he or she refuses to engage in discussion with someone whose religious beliefs are different? Why or why not? What might be another reason someone would not want to discuss differing religious beliefs?
- How can we maintain humility while speaking with boldness?
- How can we be faithful Christians in a pluralistic society?

Life Application

Say:

Think of someone who has different beliefs than you do on one or more issues. Perhaps this person votes differently than you do, identifies as gay or lesbian, is a skeptic, or is of a different church or faith. Set up a coffee or lunch with this person and explore their understanding of openness, tolerance, pluralism, and the belief that Christians are judgmental. Tell this person that you are participating in this study and want to listen and learn from him or her concerning the ideas of openness, tolerance, pluralism, and nonjudgmentalism.

Keep in mind that your purpose is to listen and understand, not lecture and persuade. Embody for this person the love of Christ. Listen as though you were lending this person "the ear of God." Ask the Holy Spirit to guide your conversation. If you are asked for your perspective, give it, or politely ask if this person would be willing to listen to your thoughts. Agree on a time to begin and end your conversation, and respect those limits.

After completing this exercise, think of ways you can better love your neighbor as a disciple of Jesus, asking him to teach you.

Closing the Session (10 Minutes)

A Final Reflection

Say:

As Christians, we believe there is an eternal fact, the fact of Christ, and an absolute standard of truth—the Holy Trinity. We believe that all authority belongs to Christ, and that his Kingdom shall have no end. Our understanding of openness, tolerance, other religious traditions, and moral judgments must take on a Christlike shape. In the present age, we may face persecution and hardship for how this is undertaken, but we should not be surprised. He told us this would happen. Therefore, we shall not fear but place our confidence in his righteousness, unapologetically showing his great love for all people, even those who would disagree with us or seek to kill us. We worship a God who loved our world so fully he laid down his life to secure our salvation. Christ has redeemed us by his grace. We are free to love freely. This is an eternal fact and an absolute truth we can bet our lives on.

Closing Prayer

Almighty, holy, and loving God, we are in need of a new heart. Make us into people who are so loving, so accepting, so truthful, so graceful, so bold, and so gentle that our world might revel in your beauty. Your absolutes are superior to our ideas of civility; your love and justice surpass our best efforts at governance and public life. May your kingdom come, quickly, in us. Amen.

Session 6
What Does Love Require?

Charting the Course

Learning Objective

Participants will synthesize grace and truth as inseparable elements of life as disciples of Jesus, and they will be encouraged to devote their lives to the pursuit of that synthesis revealed fully in Christ.

Themes for Exploration

- What did Jesus mean when he said his disciples were to be "the salt of the earth"?
- What does it mean to love?
- What is the meaning of repentance? How are we called to repent? How do we faithfully call others to repentance?
- After six sessions, how have we grown in our understanding of what it means to be a person of grace and truth?

Key Scripture

I keep asking that the God of our Lord Jesus Christ, the glorious Father, may give you the Spirit of wisdom and revelation, so that you may know him better.

Ephesians 1:17

Theological Focus

"If we're going to be salt, if we're going to make this world a better place as Jesus said we should, then we need to possess both grace and truth just as Jesus did. We must have compassion for people and passion for truth—not one instead of the other or one more than the other, but both together in equal measure."

Getting Started (10 Minutes)

Opening Prayer

Lord Jesus, you came to our earth full of grace and truth. As your disciples, you have called us to follow your example; but we confess we err, failing to embody a synthesis of grace and truth. Help us to strike the right balance. Give us the grace we need. Make us holy. We love you, and we ask these things in your name. Amen.

Conversation Starter

Ask:

What is the most significant insight you have gained through your participation in this study?

Alternate Option: Look for a story online that serves as an example of compassionate love in action. Share the story or show the video clip. Ask group members how the individual(s) in this story demonstrate the kind of love we see in Christ.

Engaging the Material (40 Minutes)

Note: This section allows approximately 25 minutes total for discussion (of video, Scriptures, and book). More questions are provided than you will have time to cover; select in advance those questions you would like to discuss, putting a check mark beside each one.

The Video

Play: Session 6: What Does Love Require? (running time 13:25)

Discuss:

- Why do you think our culture tends to think that the loving thing to do should always make others feel good?
- Why is it so important for us to walk the way that Jesus walked? What is at stake if we do not get the balance of grace and truth right?
- How does understanding and accepting God's love and grace set us free? What does this have to do with balancing grace and truth?
- What does it mean to make the truth plain? How do we do this? How is this what love requires?
- Do you believe that we can redeem our culture by balancing grace and truth as Jesus did?

The Scriptures

In Advance: Use a commentary or Bible dictionary to help you prepare for this segment. Become familiar with the text before the group session. Write down your own discussion questions in addition to those provided below.

Read: Ephesians 1:15-23

Ask:

- How does Paul extend grace to the church at Ephesus? What is his hope for them? How might we have a similar heart for others?

- What does it mean for disciples to receive "the Spirit of wisdom and revelation"? How might this help us as we seek truth?
- What is "the riches of [God's] glorious inheritance" and "[God's] incomparably great power for us who believe" in Christ? What might these things teach us of God's grace?
- How should Christ's exalted position above "all rule and authority, power and dominion" simultaneously humble us and instill confidence in us?
- Paul writes that Christ is the head of the church. What might this mean for our relationships with Christians with convictions that differ from our own?

The Book

Chapter 6 brings our study to a close with an exploration of the requirements of love. Grace and truth, properly combined, result in love. We have seen this most fully in Christ. Even when Christ spoke a hard word of truth, it was an act of grace. He could have let the wayward person continue on a path to destruction, but he did not. God's desire is for humankind to experience his love.

To share God's love to our friends and neighbors, we must follow Jesus' teaching and example. This is a challenge. Faithful discipleship to Jesus requires grace and truth. As Jesus says in Matthew 5:13, we are called to be the "salt of the earth." This means we are to be in relationship with those in our communities, extending grace and humbly presenting the truth we have found in Christ.

Discuss:

- What does it mean for us to be the "salt of the earth"? If we are to be salt in this way, why is it essential for us to have compassion for people and passion for truth in equal measure?

- When has standing for the truth in a postmodern culture brought you criticism or charges of being narrow-minded, mean-spirited, or unloving? How can we encourage one another in the face of opposition?
- Share a painful decision that love has caused you to make. Why was it difficult? Why did you make it? What was the result of your decision?
- Respond to this statement concerning divisions in the church: "What we need most is not a discussion that attacks each other's motives but a dialogue that helps us understand what love is and what it requires from us as followers of Jesus." Do you agree? Why or why not? How do we achieve this?
- How does choosing only grace or truth keep us from balancing our faith and representing Christ well? What practices help us to grow in both grace and truth?
- What do you believe that love requires?
- After six sessions, how have you grown in your understanding of what it means to be a person of grace and truth?

Life Application

Say:

Grace and truth, embraced together as indispensable facets of following Christ, should result in acts of great love. It is not enough for us to simply hear God's Word concerning grace and truth. We must put it into practice.

Do not let this study of grace and truth lead solely to a different way of thinking. Put what you have learned into action. Here are some suggestions:

- Continue to grow as someone who listens. Practice with your family and friends.

- Pool financial resources with other Christians and support a worthy cause.
- Collect clothing items for the needy.
- Walk through your neighborhood and pick up trash.
- Deliver a meal to someone recovering from illness.
- Volunteer to read to children at an underresourced school.
- Brainstorm other ideas.

Strive to be a person who does justice, loves mercy, and walks humbly with God (see Micah 6:8).

Closing the Session (10 Minutes)

A Final Reflection

We read in John 1:14, "The Word became flesh and made his dwelling among us. We have seen his glory, the glory of the one and only Son, who came from the Father, full of grace and truth." Jesus' words were not only truthful and gracious. These qualities were on display in the totality of his life. Every action. Every thought. The inclination of his heart. The posture of his body toward every person he encountered. He placed that kind of character into the community he formed around himself. It is a grand vision, but God has chosen to give witness to himself by placing the life of Christ in us, visible signposts to the reality of God's kingdom. May we ask God for help in becoming people full of grace and truth, and may we boldly act in faith, trusting the Holy Spirit to make it so.

Closing Prayer

Almighty God, we close our study in prayer, in the same manner with which we began. We seek to be faithful disciples of Jesus.

May we behold him, filled with grace and truth. May we see that in him, a life is possible where compassion and righteousness, love and holiness, and justice and mercy, can be held in tandem. Help us to hold fast to his teachings and to follow his example. In Jesus' name. Amen.

Optional Activities
for Enhancing the Study

The following are optional activities for enhancing the overall learning experience of this six-week study.

1. Light a Christ Candle

As you begin each session, light a candle. Make sure the candle has enough life to last the duration of your session.

Read John 1:1-5, 14 aloud at the beginning of each session:

In the beginning was the Word,
and the Word was with God,
and the Word was God.

He was with God in the beginning.

Through him all things were made;
without him nothing was made that has been made.

In him was life,
and that life was the light of all mankind.

The light shines in the darkness,
and the darkness has not overcome it.

The Word became flesh
and made his dwelling among us.
We have seen his glory,
the glory of the one and only Son,
who came from the Father,
full of grace and truth.

Say:

We have seen the Lord Jesus, full of grace and truth. We ask for his help. May we learn from you, O Lord. Fill us with your grace and your truth. Amen.

2. Serve a Communal Meal

If you plan a 90-minute session, incorporate a communal meal as part of the experience. If you meet at a church building and your group is small enough to manage the expense, have people sign up to bring food for everyone as part of your study. Alternatively, pool your resources and prepare something inexpensive, such as hot dogs or crock-pot dishes, for a main course. If your meeting is later in the evening, bring small desserts or snacks. Or, rotate host homes of members in your study. I have seen each option work with a variety of groups. Eating together fosters community and increases a sense of belonging to one another.

3. Plan a Cultural Outing to Spark Discussion

After Session 3 (Worldviews), plan an outing to a movie, a play, or an art museum. Do a little research on the film, play, or art exhibit prior to your outing. After the viewing, meet for coffee or dessert. Discuss what you observed. Which worldview was on display? What claims were made concerning truth? Did you discover a message of grace?

4. Conduct Interviews on Attitudes Toward Truth and Grace

Have study participants conduct interviews with friends, neighbors, and coworkers on attitudes toward truth and grace. (This survey might be conducted between Sessions 1 and 2, though it could be done at any time during the study.) Ask each participant to interview three people. Seek diversity—seek people of other generations or cultures.

Have participants ask the following questions:

- What is truth?
- How do we decide what is true and false?
- Do you believe there are some things that are true in all times and in all places? Why or why not?
- Do you believe that it is OK to offer someone a second chance? In what situations? Is there ever a time someone should not be offered a second chance? Why?
- Do you think that our culture leans toward truth or grace? Why?

Allow additional time during one of the sessions for sharing and discussing the interview responses, or plan a time outside of the regular group sessions for getting together and discussing the experience.

5. Encourage the Discipline of Not Having the Last Word

A story is told of a professor of philosophy who also was a Christian. One day in class the professor was challenged very strongly by one of his students. After listening to this student's perspective, the professor simply said, "Thank you. That is all for today. We are dismissed. I will see you next time." Another student asked the professor, "Why didn't you let that guy have it? You could've easily refuted his position." The professor replied, "I am practicing the discipline of not having the last word."

Recommend this discipline as an additional Life Application one week. While it important for us, as Christians, to know and proclaim the truth, there also is a time to listen and remain silent. Sometimes not having the last word is an act of grace.

Notes

1. Blaise Pascal, *Thoughts,* accessed at Bartleby.com: http://www.bartleby.com/48/1/14.html.
2. Leslie T. Lyall, *A Passion for the Impossible: The Continuing Story of the Mission Hudson Taylor Began* (London: OMF Books, 1965), 37; accessed online at OMF International: http://www.omf.org/omf/us/resources__1/omf_archives/famous_china_inland_mission_quotations/hudson_taylor.
3. Anne Lamott, *Bird by Bird: Some Instructions on Writing and Life* (New York: Pantheon, 1994), 22.